Waking Bodies

Waking Bodies

poems

REX WILDER

Red Hen Press Los Angeles

Waking Bodies

Cover art by Michi Colacicco
        Untitled, 2005
        Mixed media on paper
        9" x 12"

Book design by Michael Vukadinovich
Cover Design by Mark E. Cull

ISBN: 1-59709-062-X (tradepaper)
ISBN: 1-59709-065-4 (clothbound)

Library of Congress Catalog Card Number: 2005933781

Published by Red Hen Press

The City of Los Angeles Cultural Affairs Department, California Arts Council, Los Angeles County Arts Commission and National Endowment for the Arts partially support Red Hen Press.

First edition

for

Robert Sallin

Judy Briskin

Jessica Hornik, my partner in rhyme

Angela, Madeline, Simon & Oliver

Acknowledgments

The American Poetry Review: "Six-Thirty"; *The Antioch Review*: "Drought Notes," "Foreword," "Romeo of Séverine," "Séverine and Her Trophy Flower"; *Colorado Review*: "The Flood," "The Last Ten Minutes," "Southernmost Love Poem"; *Los Angeles Review*: "Le Presbytère"; *L.A. Weekly*: "In and Outback"; *The Nation*: "Sounding Aboard the *Rafaella*"; *The New Republic*: "The Baby"; *Poetry*: "René Underground," "Séverine in Summer School"; *Poetry Ireland Review*: "Normandy Redivivus," "How He Loved Her"; *Slope*: "Séverine at the Albergo Ristorante"; *Southern Review*: "&," "The Folder"; *Times Literary Supplement*: "Cedars of Lebanon," "The Key," "Séverine's Ark," "Violé"; *Yale Review*: "For S., Whom I Did Not Marry"; *Yellow Silk*: "The Balcony," "Séverine Between Marriages."

"The Balcony" was reprinted in *Yellow Silk: The Book of Eros*.

"&," "The Baby," "For S., Whom I Did Not Marry" and "Séverine in Summer School" reappeared on the "Poetry Daily" website.

"The Baby" was featured in the *Poetry Daily: 366 Poems from the World's Most Popular Poetry Website* anthology.

"Séverine Between Marriages" received an Honorable Mention from the Pushcart Prize.

"Séverine in Summer School" was a Featured Poem on the *Poetry* magazine website.

Contents

The Blueprint Sky

The Space of Ten Dozen Lawns

. . . as the sun acknowledges
With a warm look the world's hunks and colors,
The soul descends once more in bitter love
To accept the waking body . . .

—RICHARD WILBUR,
"Love Calls Us to the Things of This World"

Waking Bodies

The Sign Says November There

Geese have the long arms of romantic heroes.
They go courting to Canada and back.
And don't we wonder what sustains us,
Meat separating from bone in the stew
Of time. In the radiance of a naked body,
You can read these words without your glasses:
Cry if you must, but let it be a lover's moan.
If you have to be weak, let it be like a flower-stalk,
Which falls on its knees in the rain.

A Beautiful Strain

Séverine in Summer School

Naked for twenty-four of our last thirty-six
Hours together, and I mean museum-quality, sex-
Shop, God-riddling naked, sapping gold
Light from the windows of her hundred-year-old
Baltimore dorm, we were hungry for selling
Points, like a couple in a showroom. Compelling
Arguments were made to close the deal
And children were discussed. I kissed her from heel
To head in a shower without water;
Then with. Nude, she read me a letter as a waiter
Would his specials, and I couldn't keep
My eyes off: smooth shoulders, belly, pelvis,
Deep olive skin all a balm against sleep.
It was from her sexy grandmother in Dieppe
And Séverine translated, both of us
Somehow drawn to this third party in a tidal
Sort of way, her lunar candor, her antipodal
Ease with words and the world. We were difficult,
Séverine and I, a beautiful strain, a cult
Of two. Even eating, we made lots of noise.
Even resting in bed, watching the trees,
Our lighter breathing, our limb-shifting, sheet-
Rustling, even our dreaming had fight.
Her heart was exceptionally loud—not with love,
But with knowing. Knowing what to be afraid of.

Violé

It was like the cartoon dog who accelerates
To break down the door, but the cat waits
Behind and opens it when the dog's an inch
Away and the dog sails past his lunch
To a far wall and their masters' finest plates.
It was so easy, and silly. And it does not
Matter much whether we were dog or cat.

Pre-Raphaelite

We'd be weeds
If trees looked down
But they don't.
We serve the needs
Of no one
They know,
And won't.
We water and prune
And scatter seeds
But God knows He
Can do that
On his own.
So why do we lie
After love
By the reeds
And feel so very
Important?

Sounding Aboard the Rafaella

She loved me as the freeloading sea
Gulls love the slipstream of a mammoth hull.
It was her passion, this lack of need for me.
She let her resistance fall like an empire, her clothes like a tyrant's
Head: momentous and kindling, like no fire since.

And I loved her in the lull
Between vessels, in the tenselessness of an unbroken
Breaker, in the two mouths where one tongue was spoken.
The freighter's engine throbs against its cage
Of ocean, and my heart wrecks against this page.

Séverine Between Marriages

Séverine was writing letters
Instead of using the telephone.
The snoopy ex-music teacher
Across the way probably guessed
Suicide.

The sweat beading Séverine's forehead and temples,
Though, was not a sign of distress, but of her mind,
At its turning point, letting go.

The first months of her thirty-first year
Had been spent finding the holes
In arguments, and then looking for something
To fill them with.

If you can believe the romances,
Séverine had received the gift
Of her physical beauty in installments,
And the instructions had been,
Until now, inexplicably withheld.

Séverine's letters described in detail plans for her
Now unplannable future. They began so energetically
A reader might have thought she'd had a head start,

A page before page one, but then they would peter out, or actually
In, into her next top-heavy attempt to let the world know what
She suddenly didn't.

The day Séverine took the bundle of correspondence
To the post office, the walk home took on the significance
Of the fall of Rome: all roads led, for once, away.

Higher and lower orders clashed in a series of spontaneous demonstrations,
And, with the flourish of an international accord, a sweeping lack
Of understanding was reached. Impressions, in this new atmosphere,
Assaulted Séverine: were they trying to sell her something?
The mud scent in the Tuileries, for example, didn't stop at wafting;

It badgered her until she, feeling as if she'd just come into a good
Deal of money, bought the whole park.

She took more
And more
Showers, especially
On rainy days,
When the steady
Stream
That pelted her
Felt echoed,
As if all of Paris
Were as naked
As she, its every
Component,
Like a bicycle
Spoke, spinning
Out delight
In all directions.

She loved the way her body
Could be so easily slapped
To attention.

   She opened
Her mouth
   Her arms
Her legs

. . . and took the city in. She put the city on.

She put other people in all her places.

She hummed along with ambulances.

She ran her fingers over the slightly oily muscles

Of public statues

Of famous people

As if she knew them.

She ate fewer meats, and took long walks on the weekends
Through the farmlands near her family's country home outside of Luneray,
Marveling at the damp soil and the touching, week-by-week yielding
Of innocence on the part of the crops,
Especially the Calvados apples and the beautifully strewn

Dieppoise potatoes. Her last weekend in Normandy
She celebrated her birthday with friends and her ex-husband's friends,
All of whom noticed the change in her. And although the sound
Was drowned out by the popular music on the record player,
Séverine heard ripe fruit fall through stars to the ground.

Her rebellion was private,
And consisted in braless,
Sprightly walks home from work,
When the most intimate
Centrifugal forces could disport
Themselves beneath her blouse,
And in wearing short
Blue jean skirts sans underwear,
Millimeters between the breezes
That touched her and those
That touched the rest of mankind.

She couldn't explain it, didn't want to.
Opening the door to her apartment foyer
Was as enjoyable as eating a fragrant pastry,
And she would linger at both,
Celebrating entrances.

Séverine had always slept with nothing on,
But in a fetal position.

Now she woke mornings spread open
Like a palm leaf, as if the fan of her own desire.

She looked at herself in these moments,
The golden, indeterminate shadows
Making their points at every part of her,
And she ran her fingers, as if dialing
A telephone, over the thousands of possible
Combinations.

Every morning
A new number,
A new response.
Every morning
The same ring
Ringing differently
In a new house
That no one had
Ever lived in.

Séverine felt
as if
she were
sharing
her body
with a hummingbird
and
that all she
had to do

was relentlessly find flowers.

Séverine at the Albergo Ristorante

An early shower the morning after a storm
And a desperate craving for coffee on the terrace.
Vapors rising from the brilliant lake's surface.
The iron slatted chairs still wet where the wind
Blew in the rain from the west. No waiters anywhere.
The earth writing me down like a journal entry,
Trying to write me in before I'm out. Me, unbearably
Happy. *To love well*, I tell Thirst, my companion,
Is to live in mourning for the living. Why bother
With sunrise if not to put the darkness behind us,
To lavish attention on what wakes up, too?

Balcony

i.

Her tongue-traveled-upon torso arches
    Inches ahead of the looming
Flicker, in praise of it, like a crowd's
    Progressive ovation, assuming
The lead runner's arrival; or jasmine,
    Anticipating night, blooming—

ii.

If light could slide down your sleeping breasts like water, or the moon
Drop needles on the sea . . . — A mourning dove: *Too soon, soon, soon.*
The perfect note cannot stand on its own. Hence memory, the tune.

—Port-la-Galère

Romeo of Séverine

In our most bird-like moments, wings
Rarely enter our imaginings.
Perched here, she clings

To me as if I were a branch on the tree
Of forever and says things
Like "Don't go" and "Stay inside me"

As rivers do to springs
That feed them, and leaving one knee
Over her, I hedge temporality.

Chaste

Her lips are, well, Impressionist
And forward, and appeared to roam
Ever so slightly as the last
Sleep left my eyes, while sun
Divided monarchies of dust
To humble the silver and gild the toast.
He swore he'd been kissed
When she called him to breakfast
From across the room.

—Arques-la-Bataille

Le Presbytère

Desperation: no medley or melody, nothing symphonic
　　　In the pell-mell bird-noise or even mnemonic,
Nothing you'd even *want* to remember for that matter,
　　　Notes pecking at noteworthy, a Satur-
Day night university bar scene on a weekday morning
　　　In a jacaranda tree. Then, without warning,
The flock cleared, perhaps adjoined to the pretty objects
　　　Of their desire; but whether sky or sex,
Wanderlust, fawning, or even playfulness lay behind
　　　The sudden vacancy and silence, I found
Your voice there, and talk of breakfast, simple words—
　　　And was glad to be rid of the pompous birds.

In and Outback

On my back, on her bed.
A lorikeet tipping into guava nectar
By the window was an altar
Beneath which she said
Nothing for hours with her mouth.
Never been this far south.
The outback, the in her.
Her breasts were my breaths
Made tangible; when I held
Them, I passed out: little deaths.

&

Do I have to spell it out? *And* is a grand-
Parent or sacred text, respect on demand
Certainly, a star on every language's
Hollywood Boulevard, but no teenager's
First choice when heady impatience
Walks into the room, her future tense
All beguilement. Eternity's stunt double,
Space with impeccable timing, trouble
Looked forward to: the ampersand insists
On promiscuity, on strangers' trysts,
No previous likeness necessary until later,
When they get to know each other better.
One line, one pick-up line to prove
No match is inconsequential, or love.

Bertolucci Discovers Séverine

Halfway across the   country, the continent
Divides, sorting rain   and melting snow,
Pronouncing rivers,   filling maps; water's bent
And snapped over   the knee of Colorado.
Seeing all, my lust   settles on her still-wet
Hair, which parts   easily, and falls into the sun
On one side; on the   other, into none.
Every moment is a   watershed, or not.

Séverine's Ecstasy

I am the tree
in the yard
who can watch
the wood burn
in the fireplace
and do nothing
because I am
a tree in the yard.

Séverine's Neighborhood

Life goes on for some and not for others.
Life goes on for others and not for some.
Some of the others go on with their lives.

Séverine's E-Mail

I was the Speeding Beauty
To your Green Light;
I sped past you without a thought,
On my way to some holy city.

Séverine's Ark

An alarmist mist builds up beyond the zoological park,
Wanting rain from the horizon.
The Victorian architecture is prudish.
The brick is painted navy blue,
And who cannot think of that lonely ship running
Its epoch-making errand for God?

The first time it was because the world was too wild.
The second because there is not wilderness enough.

Inside, a polar bear, contained steam,
Her pelt panted over in a declaration of pure animal,
Lets her cage-mate lift off her slowly—
Not like a ghost, but a ghost's opposite.
She blinks the incandescent light away,
Which catches the future in a dew-drop on his penis.

Séverine and Her Trophy Flower

I was distracted from the roses by an ugly flower.
Actually, by an attractive local who was smelling it.
Stem bent into a letter of introduction. Ill-curled
Bloom surprising me with the fragrance of its neglected gasp,
A wholly unrosy odor I could almost devour.
What happened then? Perhaps a quiet, telling rite
Of calibration, beauty refining its grasp
On me. I stepped out of my country into the world.

—Parc Floral des Moutiers

A Winter Wedding

The bride says

In my happiness, the tight
Clench of my eyes, that their lids
Might be sewn shut
Against the sight of time passing.

The groom responds

A descendant of a moth caught
By the light of time passing
In September's porch weather has no thought
Of flight now.

Number Ten

Nights on end of dreamlessness.
Responsible, unresponsive sleep.
Three weeks going on years.
Hill Street, with no aspirations
To graduate or diminish.
Only this human rise: six feet,
Barely perceptible over a quarter
Mile. A hell street to winter on.
It begins in general (a general
Store) and ends on the strength
Of a dead end, that barrier
From which no surprise ever
Advances. No one comes back
From the dead. Not even you.

Normandy Redivivus

I always meant to go back, to loll in salty maritime
Museums sailed through on my inaugural voyage,
To socialize with the local Communists, who have time

To spare, to collect the rewards a boy aged
Thirty promised the man who returned him home,
Which was how it felt, then. Even my marriage,

Terminal, released doses of sweetness, like *les pommes*
Of Calvados and Gourel, into the bloodstream.
Even my broken French healed, churning the foam

Of sympathy. Oh squandered days! A stream
Of scribbled notes drafted in hot fury
And never played. My closed eyes form a seam

About to burst: a scene in which a cherry
Wood writing table opposite a fire
Is magnetic north spreads out from the presbytery

Where we lived, across the barbed wire
That shielded God's half-acre from our Parisian
Neighbors', and over potato fields and a briar

Heath to the castle at Arques and its moat of horizon.
I haunted there, cocksure as Hansel, the ghost
Of a chance, spirit of the chase, racing

Over the greatest possible ground; my heart embossed
With invitations and answers, full beyond reason . . .
My future, found, had been ordered, and at no cost

To me, to be held under my name (crossed
Out now) until I washed ashore on my native coast:
A shell, into which a new life crawled, almost.

Drought Notes

Drought Notes

Pressure at my temples like a balm to relieve
The pressure that preys beneath it . . .
Why would anything *want* to be understood?
I loathe not the aftermath but the moment
Of comprehension. No more pain
Gleaned from the dead run of enlightenment
(Where the sails swell but no wind is felt)
Than from the ignorant darkness . . .
That instant, that epiphanic crack is my plague,
And the echoing thud—a code broken,
Like a raccoon by a car's headlit prow, and thrown
Open for all to see, the spasm, the spine
Of unintelligibility thwarted, bent into some
Letter of some alphabet. The body of
Imminent knowledge, which is all innocent life,
Supports its cargo in secrecy, and so naturally
Craves the shadows that prolong it.

Here lies the lover's lesson, and the rocket
Ship's, too, from within whose elaborate
Scaffolding the first *I love you* is jettisoned out
Of time into space. Flight is black and white,
Feet are either firmly planted on the ground
Or not. So it was in the beginning, my own
Feet very much land-locked and restless
At the state-owned and -operated parking lot's edge . . .

The freshly painted asphalt surrendered
To the weed-rich red Georgia clay
Like a second to a first, more formidable
Wife, the one with the kids. The trails,
Evidently to weed out the less serious hiker,
Were marked blue and red, easier and more
Difficult, like arteries and veins in the body

Of a spring-wakening forest, but it was
A third branch of trails, one more suited
To goats or death-wishers and marked off
By yellow posts like the faithful who cheer
Their wrongly accused and convicted
Champion along the road to prison, that
Decided me.

My seduction had less of Frost to it than Faust.

The first days of a drought always pass
Like contemporaries of no particular
Beauty or distinction who will later become famous,
Mobbed and asked for
Autographs wherever they go.

What lured me to the waterfall was the fall
Itself, the sheer serial plunges and dropoffs
Even the unrelieved Earth (an inexorable
Handicap ramp of a slope to Key West
Eight hundred miles away) seemed grateful for.
The time, not just to think, but of things,
And the warm space such conception requires,
I crave adulterously,

                      and as I proceeded down
The path to my destination, each succeeding
Signpost was like a removed garment
Tossed at my feet. I came to my senses, which
Always seem to be waiting for me in places like this,
As suddenly as if brakes had been applied.
When I stopped, everything that claimed citizenship
To the past, friends, relatives—all my dead,
The illegitimate, legitimizing memories which
Had been trailing me and fighting
For position like bicyclists in the draft
Of an eighteen-wheeler
Truck, surged past me, and disappeared.

Dogwoods. Squint and the bract-blossoms
Stagger across your liberated vision's plane
Like a late city's surviving lit windows.

If every window winds up making light
Of whoever draws it blinds, two weeks
From now each flower will abandon

Its branch, and illuminate the earth it lands on.

The azalea-scented, dogwood-studded glades
Gave way then, like now, to this resort
Of ferns, where the youngest members of the oldest
Phylum disport themselves with neither
Modesty nor motion, their one-piece suits
Rolled down to their waists as they soak
In the pine, fir, oak, and tulip-tree shadows
Beside what passes, provided I confine
My gaze to the hours between eleven and one,
For a mountain pool. I don't think about
Work.

A month later, last flower over, summer
Beginning to add up. The dogwoods evict us
From the present, only to move us
Into a more expensive tense. Denied the beeches'
Or the maples' fullness, fulfillment
(June, July, August) eludes them.
They hang out leaves from their foolish
Limbs like "Now Leasing" signs.

Drought, too, throws us out, into remembered rain.

Days dogged by days, of so little wasted
Motion as to suggest winter, and night.

This summer, rain is the romance novel
All nature is reading. Even so, the burgeoning
Waist of Angel's Creek (how can it be?)
Makes me hope for depth, and life beneath
The surface. Leaves forced to confront
October before Labor Day break down,
Making soggy, repeated attempts to assimilate.
Breadth, as if chinning up to a bar,
Strains to equal length but cannot contain
Itself for long. Beyond the ferns,
Beneath the sun, the modest stream pulls
Its clouded hood over the hundred-foot plunge
And accelerates in one roared and repeated
Word of tribute, beginning in *oh* and ending in
Shhh, to the nearby Chattahoochee, so shallow
A city river as never to be bored with praise.

"It's only a dog—"

                         A high-pitched sound,
Whether the enthusiasm of a startled thing
Or the scrape of disparate elements,
Any screech that resisted easy identification
(Those Chinese firs—behind them—
A halting train?) used to bring
My tragicomic epileptic cocker spaniel Zelda to mind.
She's having another seizure,
I'd think, and tilt my head to calculate
The path my rescue would take.

Now she's gone I rest easy.

Where some resort to lopsided risk
To keep their poise in, I make geometry:
My losses, confined, and plotted
Along the x axis of my felt history,
Free compensation up to wait
Along the y and the z, like the same
Commuter at opposite ends of the day,
Or a meal in the freezer, or a seed.

The mathematical improbability staggers me,
That I should be so, on the one hand,
Drawn, and on the other, rebuffed by the demands
My loved and living ones make on me,
Scattered as they are, their claims on my heart
So unequal, as to have nothing else to do
But loiter here, with not a strain on a muscle.

Poise is all I can expect,
When every decision is
A close vote in Parliament
And the contest leaves
Both sides' authority in
Question.

I think of the mind that a monument closes.
A far cry from a Parthenon or even art-deco drive-in,
I echo their sentiments. Spectators arrive in
Memory, like days without you. Everything goes as

Planned, or doesn't. The architect and inspiration move
On once a monument is up and staying.
"Child." Try saying
That ten thousand years in a row. I'm spending old love.

Angela

Awakened by rain, I lay my head
Down sideways to meet the rise of her breath
And carefully fall with it,
Like foam on a wave, my ear
On the slight swell below
Her waist. Heaven has chosen to pitch its next tent here.
I listen in: *Take the heartbeat on faith,*
The gods seem to say, *As only your prayers*
Will be answered. — Trust the stealth
Of the new life inside. In a sense, it's all over.
The genetic trading floor that decided
The impetuous cell, our son or daughter whom luck
Will fit for a century, is empty.

Our family trees are lashed by relief.

The Blueprint Sky

The Flood

i.

A forest that from drivers' and passengers' points of view
Flourishes four or five states of mind deep turns out,
When viewed from overhead, to be, at best, a moustache
Drawn above each lip of America's parkways and under
Time's nose. No, let's make the metaphor the two
Fingers of a Cub Scout's pledge (the trees) in which
The space that extends beyond the oath
(The unembellished world) is so far removed from hope
That I have to switch images on you again. I'm sorry,
But I'm standing here in the dressing room of my despair
And nothing fits. Still, you must be getting the picture:
Fifty feet to the left and right of the left and right
Shoulder of every drop-dead gorgeous road in creation
And then it's all the moral of the tale. Or look at it
This way: Fewer than a hundred people in Georgia still
Speak with a Southern accent and the salt
Water of sameness is rising in them like a killer tide.

ii.

Let this poem be the helicopter that hovers
Over your alphabetical order. Let the glass bubble be
Large enough for every hurt you've ever endured
As you cruise over every cause and condemn it.
The rotor blades and fuel are my rage and age respectively,
So stopping to re-fuel would mean stopping to re-soul.
I'd rather crash. I do. I'm history. Listen,
Who can take a stand in public anymore without wearing
A politically correct earring of embarrassment?
The nineties are a one-scoop ice cream cone.
What's going on here? A screech of brakes in the cosmos.
Planet Earth at the turn of two thousand's been hit
And is way too hurt to be moved. Wait for the paramedics—
The metaphysics. *Hold me*, the water in every argument cries.

iii.

All I want is a little privacy.
A nature preserve for human nature.
A breeding ground.
A place where God, in peace and quiet, can nurture
A quirk into a mark of distinction, or personality, or art.

iv.

I draw the curtains to bring you the future:
It's just a matter of time before everything touches
Everything and everyone, everyone.
The fortune teller over on Cheshire Bridge is in heaven.
After the flood, she says, angels will arrive,
Less like birds alighting on a wreck
Than vacationers come to partake of (read *plunder*)
Our famous waters. They'll pack their bags
Just as our fates' need to be sealed invokes the cold,
Stay long enough to perform figure-eight
Infinities on the frozen surface, and be off.
So let's hear it for the boy with his finger
In the dike and the international dam industry,
But by no means invest in either.

v.

Tonight, the tender words exchanged
By the two of us in our native language
On this living room sofa would be
The rubber stopper in extinction's sink,
Except that the language itself is full
Of holes. Nuances escape us
Like the animals nobody talks about
Who jumped Noah's ship—and only
Our kisses float on mute reflection.

Outpost

Allow me all or nothing,
Allow me to surpass love,
Allow me.
Drop me off at eternity's curb
And I will make things up.
I will make a life for myself.
I will bind the primer of invention.
Motionless already,
I will not know where to stop,
The way Creation
Without restraint left Alaska alone.
No further,
Higher, lower,
Brighter, more perfectly chiseled
Or grand?
Out of thin air I produce
A pair of snow geese,
Knowing I must be left behind.
And as they glide past
In slow-motion
High speed, their long necks migrate
Hours into the future,
Where my bicycle
Still rests, propped against
The spruce.
Everywhere else glaciers
Either inch forward or back.
Matanuska doesn't move.
And if I died here, without you
Or you, the ice
Would study my bones like a painter
A bowl of apples.
I would never be swept away.

The Last Ten Minutes

I am the greatest nation on earth and into me melt
A hundred epochs of ice, the calming skin of the water come to rest
In a motionless glass, water, that will, when swallowed,
Make my own flesh a kind of interior
And demand of the air in the room and the buildings across the street
And the swaths of forests coursing like rivers
Between former forests and the rivers themselves that they be
My heart and my head. I am the greatest nation on earth and into me melts
The smell of the rose on the table whose display was delayed
Until after its move from soil to vase—a rose I removed from the earth
Of which I am, by virtue of style, the greatest nation.
The sky will soon apply inside me for permission to proceed.
Birds (read *impressions made*) will move
Stage left to right in iambs past my setting sun,
Blue as veins coming, red as arteries going,
The sole but substantial wind created by their alternating m, v, m, v, m, v,
Though those letters too will collapse in the absence of vowels
(Read *soul*), to be replaced by draftless gliding parallel continuous lines.
The white space time cannot black in or out
Is how these lines hold sway. Into me melts the mind of the water
On the lip of the glass that chaperones the poison.
Thick, deliberate, irreversible, the mind of the water conducts my thoughts
Like the last ferry of the season on a northern lake.
I show my gratitude by dying before I reach the other side.
May my successors enjoy the circuitous winter detour.

René Underground

(René, one of the twelve angels allotted to the nine
planets of the solar system, receives a grant that pays
for his trip to and from Malibu, California, plus all
the expenses incurred during his year-long internship,
during which he performs certain feats and makes
occasional mistakes.)

So the angel, accustomed to, and long ago fed up with, his taxing
And unromantic reliance on wings, lost track of time
Burrowing beneath the unstable clay, cavorting, if you will,
With the indigenous gophers. This is easy to imagine.
If you received an invitation signed in the unmistakable scrawl
Of an owl one evening, would you say no to his offer
Of a fully chaperoned and (with any luck) bloodless high-altitude mousing,
Even though you had a hundred and one chores
To do around the house? The yuccas, who would later surprise
The whole of Malibu Canyon with their sudden burst into prominence
The weekend before the Independence Day holidays, courtesy
Of a not-as-ashamed-as-he-should-have-been
Angel whose job it had been (and still was!) to push
Their candelabra-like stalks into the sky and paper them with flowers
That always turned out to be miniature versions
Of his wings in moonlight—the yuccas, who were called by postcard writers
"Our Lord's Candles" for the way they looked
When the flame of their flower was highest and for the way they flowered
Just before the flame was snuffed and the yucca died—
The yuccas, like it or not, were out of luck,
And would have, until the charms of the underground wore off
For the angel, or he was bitten by a rattlesnake, or the urge
For a breath of fresh air, to wait. For now, he savored the difficulty
Of movement, the drag of the laurel sumac roots on his ailerons,
The brownness deeper than any lack of light
That could not but overwhelm him who was bored to tears

With the lacy, doily life of an angel and the adjectives
Assigned to him as part of his job that were never very far from "opalescent"...
The crawling made him dream. The creeping made him weep.
He didn't care that his wings were tattered
Like clouds breaking up after a storm, that his mouth full of poetry
Was breathless with broken-up rock and unrealized seed.
He had often secretly prayed to gophers. He was kissing one now.

The Space of Ten Dozen Lawns

At last the kids are grown, away at X
University or making Y city their own.
There's a For Sale sign on your lawn.
Will you or will you not welcome
The fresh parents still smelling of sex?

Holiday Special

The Macy's Thanksgiving Day Parade stops
Right in front of us, as my wife props
Our new baby at her breast to feed.
The printouts on our bracelets read
Monday's date. A daisy on the breakfast tray.
Our window refuses all L.A.;
It wouldn't open for God. Giant balloons sift
Through New York's light rain and lift
The planet ever so slightly, as if cheating
A scale. I'm safe in here, eating
My carryout cafeteria omelette, excused
From work and under a spell induced
By the lack of routine. A backward Proust,
I bask in forgetting my life before today.

The Baby

"Doesn't it break your heart,"
She said to her husband one morning,
"That he's going to die one day?"

(The future, until now a silent letter, was pronounced.)

The new parents resolved to make
The present a migration towards that
Original silence, and vain
Progress was made, as if they were rowing
A boat across a lake to a restaurant
They didn't know had closed down.

Cedars of Lebanon

As heat is disputed beyond Pluto,
As a bullet fired at nothing on a desert
Will lay its head down ten, twenty
Miles away like a poppy's shadow,
So my brother is rumored to have
At once come into and gone out of
The world.
               I trace the moment
On my mother's face lifetimes later.
What broadcast cheer was born
When she saw, or was prevented
From seeing, her motionless roomer,
At her threshold and his?
She must have been smiling, despite
The hours of labor. Her smile
Must have shivered before it froze.

Young, and Yet a Relic

I try to learn the prose
    of life, but my slavish
Reproduction of its speech
    is wooden; lavish
Praise born of compassionate
    searching is all
I understand. Shall I compare
    thee? Yes.
I liken you to love you,
    to believe the loveliness
Your nakedness displays
    might be proved
By some revealing counterpart,
    might be true.
With metaphors and
    allusions, I feel for you.

The First Magnolias

He learned "happy" early for a baby,
A day or two after "apple" and three
Before Christmas, on a walk around
The block, and the sweet sound
Echoed nothing in our conversation.
It came from far away, like the Asian
Magnolias' infant blossoms
That candled ten dozen lawns
And struck me like an annunciation;
In the pronounced synonym for joy
The father was carried by the boy
On the shoulders of his spontaneity.
Happiness requires no stimulus
At all, or only December's magnolias.

The Key

I'll tell you what responsibility is.
Dusk has defeated Day in a Best of Seven
Series, and is advancing to the finals.
My wife won't be home until eleven.

My daughter's in the lifeboat
Of her bed, drifting to sleep with her first
Grownup book, a paperback about
The Titanic. Encouraging my thirst

For pattern and coincidence, ice water
On the nightstand; innocuous bergs bob
In the dark. Cats demand a waiter;
I oblige. Brain and dishwasher throb.

The hunt and capture of the wild boy
Is over in ten minutes; as always, he wins
The bottle but loses the war. "Happy day,"
He gurgles between swigs and begins

Nodding his head, with a triggered passion,
To starboard and port, as if beating
Into the wind of his own anticipation.
Our eyes, meeting and meeting,

Say a song, the song, is expected
As surely as the weather mark in a regatta.
Profanities run through my head,
Fleeing my memory's Torquemada.

I can't sing, never could, am scarred
By more than one music teacher's request
That I "mouth" the words—scared
My rebellious voice would get the best

Of the more orderly canaries
In my class. What I would give now
For the throat of a bird, to raise
A tune like a wineglass, to somehow

Toast my beautiful son on his birthday
With all the right notes. So what
If he's heard a dozen renditions to die
For already—one after today's haircut,

A barbershop quartet instigated
By a beaming Mom. Faith may not be born
In moments like this, but it
Can die, or begin to: the fabric, torn,

Unravels, is ruined like a Hardy
Heroine. Warm milk shimmers in pink
Puddles on his chin. A little Henry
The Eighth. With no more to drink,

He lobs the vessel across the room
And commands me, with his imperious
Smile, and sudden silence, to perform.
I launch myself, like a toad for Sirius . . .

This is what responsibility is:
Knowing the right gods and having
Them owe you a couple of favors.
Living forty years never craving

Them. Surprising only yourself
When a tiny room is immersed
In a miracle of perfect pitch. Half
A minute of song to make hearts burst.

Six-Thirty

I saw a mockingbird in the pepper tree.
And he wasn't mocking. He just dripped, with leftover rain
That looked like sweat. The rest of the birds sang
Desperately; this one was dead-silent as far as the eye
Could tell, but alive with suggestion. Rodin
Would have sculpted him. His presence, posture, his pride
Of place! He should have been drowning in all
The truth-seeking and false starts, the noble birds with their noble
Intentions, but instead he purified them.
He was a distillery. I know he had a daughter someplace
And I know she was hoarse with song.
Such is the way with dads: there is a branch in every girl's
Soul reserved for perching, so that in between
Breaths they may feel the weight of us, who find our love
For them cheapened by too much sincerity.

Premium Poem

I like the flowers they have in planters at gas stations:
Switzerlands amidst warring nations;
Blameless, wasteful havens for imaginations.

Totalitarian Memory Poem

I came a long way and stayed in castles.
I'm on top of the Wall. A soldier hustles
Through the guarded Eden at my feet:
Does he want to join me or shoot
Me? It's sunset, and the colors don't compare
To the concentrated freedom in the air.

The Business of Life

I love to walk, block after block, granting distance
To the cramped, sped-past neighborhood.
I love to look, from the yard with the white picket fence
To the fenceless one with the stacked wood,
Creating a mythology that's true
For seventeen-twenty-four and seventeen-thirty-two.

I love to note, and nod, and notice
The predisposition of the voters,
How the Democratic placards go
With fussy lawns, while Republicans sow
The seeds of carefree enterprise.

I love to walk, block after block, taking steps
Left by God or the city planner for citizens
Such as myself to take, and making stops
As well, like the fallen leaves of light, tens
Of thousands of them, that day and night rake
And remove. I walk and look to have a stake

In the business of life, and not just be
The taker of givens, its employee.

The Folder

Folded things speak well of you
When you're out of the room.
They hold the near future captive,
Like children about to go on recess
Or sexual pleasure at the brim of control.
I think of the pressure of your hand
Smoothing over the cloth napkin,
The bedsheet, the piece of clothing
That signal the meal to come,
The lovemaking, the spent day—
And how you stack the bath towels
As high as they'll go, as a driver
Will keep the fuel tank near full
During times of shortage. I step out
Of the shower looking to the center
Of my life, where you have folded it.
Creases will have nothing to do
With edges: It's no accident
That ledges are ledges and valleys,
So far removed from any real
Horizon, where people most often
Choose to put down roots and grow.
I like to imagine that God, who,
Faced with formlessness, folded
The world into manageable corners,
Sent me you to repeat the gesture.

Southernmost Love Poem

The hibiscus that ventures out from under
The banyan tree never looks out of sorts or bloom,
But in fact each rich red affair is a matter of a day
Or two at best, a miracle of compression
If not confusion—at once a grand opening gala
And a going-out-of-business sale—
Like the thunderstorms that hang out their staticky
Laundry beneath the cloudless tropic blue,
Or the beautiful red-haired woman who lifts
Her skirt hip-high wading out to the rocks,
Taking a walk and a swim at the same time,
Afraid to miss a thing. Even I, admiring
Her grace against the current to the point of tears,
Keep the apology that would end our quarrel
Straining on its leash. Since perfection is,
Among our imperfect kind, no more, I suppose,
Than perfect balance, our love leaves nothing
To be desired, only occasionally adjusted for,
The way the wind snaps off fresh blossoms
To make way for a restless procession of buds.

The Sad Divides

Between work and work dinner on a business trip
In a walking town and late already, I duck off Lorter Boulevard,
The direct route, and glide onto Something Lane,
Where I submit almost instantly, dreamily, to a spell of safety
Three dozen stately homes long.
The street seems blessedly drained of events.
Magnolia blossoms breathe sigh after sigh of relief,
The air conditioners drone.
I grow into my imagination.
A washed car steams in its puddled driveway.
Lighted windows broadcast the evening anchors, silenced.
The sad divides.

How He Loved Her

He thought of her as an orange, so he could hold her
Roundness in a hand perfectly molded
To her body, and peel her, and feel her sweetness

Make a mockery of his tongue, and her citrus voice
Glide happily down his throat to his heart.
He planted her like a windbreak of stiff poplars

In the Netherlands, and waited a hundred years
For this multiplication of his desire and his resolve
To reach full height, and then he slalomed

In and out of her like a boy running through a crowd
On a boulevard, so he could know her stillness
Observed from the exhilaration of full speed,

So he could be the wind itself that rustled through
Her hair, and lifted her generous arms,
Which accepted her even as he ran the other way.

He gave her the heft of megalithic
Stones and travelled six thousand years backward
To arrange her in lines and semicircles

That no one would understand, so he could watch her
Today from an automobile, and be comforted
That she has indeed survived the vicissitudes

Of progress, and can, even this far
Distanced from him, dull and overshadowed
By gorse and blue jays, move him to tears.

Foreword

The infant stands, as if rising
In court to make a motion.
We hurry to hooray, surprising
Him, this knish, our Martian

In green pajamas, this Rubens
Handful. Handsome in training,
His face's scheduled sense
Of style pulls into the station.

What, in clapping, do we wish
For him, or us? At a charity ride
Last June, I was at the finish
Line, my helmet still on, the side

Of the road lined with early
Arrivers: we ushered in the late
Ones like heroes. —He nearly
Takes his first step. It can wait,

I think. It's enough, his hand-
Over-fist reliance on the table
Leg, the blazing ascent
From the cold floor to dabble

In his future, which he wears
Lightly, like the world after Rome.
Success closes the course
It rides in on. Buoyed by the sea foam

Of our approval, he chins up,
Poses, grins—then falls,
Dashed against his own hope.
Only slightly daunted, he crawls

Away, stretching the moment
Behind him like his nation's
Flag, gift wrapping the present
In memory and patience.

For S., Whom I Did Not Marry

Turning back the years like the sheets
In the Parc Central, I give the past its due.
That is, its future. We looked down at streets
In one another's arms by the window
As if their lines formed a graph
In which x and y rose together off the page.
Now I offer this epitaph
On a bench beneath a tree that feels my age,
A tupelo, in the middle of Central Park.

Autumn this year is the girl I was good for,
Unselfconscious, exquisite, a work
Of art at play. On the city's forest floor
Lie her love-scene clothes.
She reminds herself of nothing dying,
By the looks of it. So? The throes
Of fall have always been death-defying,
The sacrifice of the leaf for the tree.
The leaf built to leave, as she did me.

The Tragedy of Merlin

His Vivien, Lady of the Lake. When
The old magician talked to her he was stalking
Himself. Like a boy, he was gawking
At self-discovery's window. Faking
Love, he thought. In this he was mistaken.

Slow

Slow, I get in the Christmas mood
Early in January. I wade in behind the tide
Of events, on time's dry sand.
In this, there seems to be some good:
My view's unique; beyond the end,
The sky itself gets off the ground.
I take the past by surprise, and goad
The resigned beast with renewed
Currency. Lived life is always sold
Half-off, cleared out, paid
Far less than full attention to. Sad,
Yes, but I fill in like a god,
With praise. This is how I get ahead:
By standing firm and falling behind.

In the Early Days

In the early days, we had to meet everywhere, and often.
Any and all places sufficed to soften
The blow of not being together: Greek coffee
Shops downtown or cafés on Columbus; at the 'Y'
After readings; on the subway and in parks;
On street corners and front stoops; on larks
And tangents, like that heron-rich train trip
Upriver to Schenectady. Seven
Days a week, we were filling up the tank of our friendship.
It was wasteful like any heaven
And eventually the intimacies we exchanged
Drew us so close, we grew deranged
With self-knowledge. In the end, I knew you no better
And myself too well, the way q knows the letter
U. You moved and I took my cue
To return to Los Angeles, to let the years renew
Us, until we were a different
Vehicle altogether—still made for transport, but efficient:
Now kingdoms cropped up from a handful of words
Scrawled across the back of museum postcards
Or spoken into a receiver. To wit, tonight: once your time zone
Reclaims you, I'm awake with
Whatever it is that loathes annihilation, perhaps the myth
Of union itself. Instead of this silence,
We'd still be talking, in the early days, running
Through details like Pamplona
Bulls until one of us died, or fell asleep mid-sentence.

From The Clear Coast

We went into the ripe woods by the sea
With metal buckets to collect guilt.
The vegetation was low, thick, sure of itself,
Into itself, a vain forest—yet the pines
Appeared deferential, and said a prayer
For us as we passed. Why, then, guilt?
Because it was, since you asked,
What this wild land was bursting with.
Was obsessed with, the way a child,
Learning his letters, sees x's, s's, and o's
On the backs of beetles, in the patterns
Of spilled toys, and in varicose veins.
Guilt ornamenting thicket, bramble, ivy.
It was guilt in berries' clothing, guilty
As sin from the summer, that left us
In a lather, as we plucked and foraged
Away. We took turns forgetting
To set the parking brake, cover the pool,
And lock up the poison, then neglected
Our loved ones in rapid fire.
We cheered each other on, since none
Of us was perfect. We didn't feel
Like predators—yet who of us so much
As loosened our hold on that creaky
Handle as we walked home in the dark,
Swinging our buckets of juicy guilt?
We had a lot to be sorry for, and tipped
Our guide accordingly.

Police Chase

"Daddy, will you play police chase
wif me? I'll learn you how and then
you can write a poem of it."
        —Simon, age 5, after dinner

I'm on
To Simon
Who uses
The Muses
Tonight
As bait.
I bite,
And half-
Regret
My poetry;
Jealous
Of Simon,
It steals
Me.

Valentino

Against the Eden green and the densities of the avocados,
High and impenetrable as planets, against a blue like Cádiz,
In the uninflected coast light and the light violet
Haze of their fellow June recruits, jacaranda blooms lit
On falling branches of air. One or two a minute,
As if they were receiving diplomas. Because the prevailing
Westerlies were quiet (it was no day for sailing),
The blossoms fell as obediently as shadows or rain
And formed a purple picture of the tree on the lawn.
Bees with the coloring of tigers seen through train
Windows pawed the soft Victorian bells. I lay on the grass
And the grass carried me, as if my body were Cleopatra's.

The Weather Never Had Time to Change

We prolong his life only a few days
But oh what days! He meets a vet, stays
Overnight with her, learns to walk
All over again and becomes the talk
Of her practice. He even earns
A reputation before he returns
To her care, this time hours cold
And in my wife's arms. "A tough old
Guy," Dr. O tells me the first time,
Sold on his release. I take him home
And the whole night November
Comes round with hors d'oeuvres
Of hope and calms my shot nerves.
For now we're everything we were.

The Gift

I have no use for your gift
But set it down gingerly
As if the slightest shift
Or bobble would bring me
Bad luck, or detonate
My love for you. A blade
Of grass from an eight-
Een-month old: one day
Maybe when you read this,
You'll know what I just
Went through. Better yet,
Perhaps I'll learn, as
The years pass, what to do
With a blade of grass.

The Far Reaches

I pace the beach like a fly
On a ribbon of syrup,
Sensitive to air and sweetness.
If I were an ancient Greek,
I'd be wearing armor against
The warrior-god Memory.
The wind, which was easy,
Like gentle Zephyrus
That propelled Ulysses close
Enough to home
That he stood on the bow
Smoothing his clothes
And checking his reflection,
Is now two or three winds.
Sand-twisters, gold-flecked,
Prove it. In a more
Serious time, they could
Have been the confounding
North, South, and East
Winds, freed when Ulysses'
Men opened a sack
In which they expected gold.
But I have no men, only
A woman and three children.
No Odysseys but indolence.
No enemy, curse,
Or fatal flaw beyond this love
Of light, that travels
Everywhere looking for me.

Summers on Woodland

Relaxation we'd later know
Sexually: premonition of afterglow
In swimming holes, in sunlight
Cut by Rousseau's forest. Coat
After sheer coat of water tried
On and rejected by the heat.
We were ten forever, tethering
Our parents' ages too; weathering
The summer thunderstorms
Of childhood, staying out of harm's
Way as we dripped and dried
Off under lemon trees, a pride
Of cubs, printed with grape leaves'
Shadows and the rest of our lives.